Saying Goodbye to Thomas

poems by

Lenora Rain-Lee Good

Finishing Line Press
Georgetown, Kentucky

Saying Goodbye to Thomas

ACKNOWLEDGMENTS

"Your Death, Rehearsed" in the September 2023 Newsletter of a Sacred Passing, a place to receive death and dying education. https://asacredpassing.org

"The Ringmaster Orchestrates the Acts" and "Guilt of the Undying" in the Fall Quarterly anthology *of Fixed and Free Quarterly,* September 2023

"Old Man at the Inipi" in *The Bride's Gate and Other Assorted Writings*, a collection by the author, Cyberwit.net, August 2021

"The feeling in the room" used with permission of his Literary Executrix, Lenora Good.

"His Bench: An Ekphrastic Poem Based on a Photograph Not Yet Taken" publicly displayed in an art show, at BARN—Bainbridge Artisan Resource Network next to a piece of wood art the poem represented to the artist, Spring 2023

Photos of Thomas by his partner Sheryl Sirotnik and his sister Sally (Sarah) Clark, used with permissions.

Special thanks to my Poetry Critique groups who provided excellent suggestions to improve the poems and the book—Alex Frankel, Bill Cushing, Robin Dunn, Will Slatterly, Dan Clark, Jim Thielman, Larry Morris. Thanks also goes to friends and fellow poets who read, commented, and proofed—Ed Stover, who knew Thomas many years ago, Giulio Magrini, Gayle Lauradunn, Marjorie Rommel.

Publisher: Leah Huete de Maines
Editor: Christen Kincaid
Cover Art: Sherry Beavers Walker
Author Photo: J.C. Penney Photography Studio
Cover Design: Elizabeth Maines McCleavy

Order online: www.finishinglinepress.com
also available on amazon.com

Author inquiries and mail orders:
Finishing Line Press
PO Box 1626
Georgetown, Kentucky 40324
USA

Contents

Photo by Sheryl Sirotnik

Photo by Sarah Clark

About Thomas and this book

I first met Thomas in 2017. We hit it off and talked about taking our relationship to a more intimate stage when he was definitively diagnosed with ALS. It takes a lot of energy to begin a new relationship, and it takes a lot of energy to die. We decided to change our relationship, before it even started, to one of Elder Brother of Choice (EBOC) and Younger Sister of Choice (YSOC)

Thomas was many things during his life—glass maker, bartender, college student, teacher—he especially liked working with and helping adjudicated kids who were headed toward the gangs and prison—silversmith, writer of stories and poems, musician, artist, publisher, sailor, world traveler. And he was curious—I don't think anything escaped his curiosity. As my EBOC, he helped me become a better writer and poet. He gave instruction without teaching or preaching. He took time to help anyone who asked.

I don't keep a journal, I write poetry, and most of these poems were written in the last year of his life, while I was with him as one of his caregivers. He read or heard most of them. And approved or changed them as asked. His poems and short stories have appeared in *Yellow Medicine Review, Red Ink, Cartier Street Review, Section 8 Magazine, Raven Chronicles, Florida Review*, and others. His ancestors were Miami, Cherokee, Irish, and English and probably others. He took great delight in telling off-color stories to his neighbors' dogs.

Thomas Hubbard died peacefully in his sleep on 30 May 2023, from ALS. His burning desire was to finish his memoir before he died. He won!

All author proceeds from this book will be equally divided between the **ALS Association** and **Death with Dignity**.

Death is not extinguishing the lamp;
it is putting out the light because the dawn has come.
—Rabindranath Tagore

Dance of the Pink Moon*

Grandmother Moon, your fullness
so bright, you burned a hole

through Grandfather Sky last night.
Or, it looks that way in my photos.

There are those who would tell me
clouds changed your shape

diffused your hard, crater-pocked edges,
gave you a soft, ethereal look.

I have never loved you more
as you graciously danced for my brother

flinging your chiffon and shimmery
veils across the heavens.

You brought him such joy last night—
possibly the last night he will gaze

upon your bright fullness.
The time nears

when you will come,
dance him to the stars

but please, Grandmother,
not soon. Not soon.

April's Full Moon, named for the pink phlox that blooms then.

His Hands: An Ekphrastic Poem Based on a Photograph Not Yet Taken

after reading the poems of Thomas Hubbard

His walk, slow, deliberate,
each foot placed just so.
Still tall, handsome in a
wild warrior way: faded copper skin,
hair cropped short, uncontrolled. He ignores
the pain as he sits, places a bag
next to him.

He smiles and nods at me.
I smile and nod back. We meet like this
most days, never speak, never touch.
He, on his bench, me on mine.

Movements determined, labored,
he opens the bag, inserts a hand,
carefully extracts crackers. He calls—
his voice gravelly, deep, strong—
Henry! Matilda!—Two crows drop
beside him. He offers
each a cracker.

Absorbed in their world
he does not notice my camera
as it moves to capture
him. His hands gnarled.
Hands of a man
who once worked hard labor
for himself, his family,
to get through life,
college, old age.

The hands of a man
who once could wield a hammer,
build a home, work the machines,
the hellishly hot machines,
that turned molten
glass into canning jars.
The hands of a man tender with his woman,

loving with their children, the
hands of a man who
once carried steel in his boot—
and knew how to protect himself,
his family, his people.

The hands of a man,
now crippled by ALS,
who once held a pen,
wrote essays and poems
for a better life, a better time,
of our people and their tribulations.

One day, he'll come, sit,
and I'll have to open the bag.
place the crackers in his hand.
But not today. Not today.

Crow Calls the Morning Storm

Stepped outside to shoot Crow
with my phone. He called,
one last time, then flew—
so, I shot a Steller's Jay for all eternity—
or however long a pixel lasts—
air is heavy, morning cool.
Silver-gray clouds
force the wet air down.

Stay out of the dark woods
if you value your soul.
Dank woods harbor succubae and daemons
find the lone traveling anima
fair to devour at their pleasure.

Rain comes today, foretold
by the Magi of NOAA. With it
comes thunder—as trolls, chased by Loki,
bowl in celestial lanes. Should Sky
Dragons elude their bindings
lightning will blindingly flash
as they toss bolts one to the other
with the occasional miss that hits Earth.

Old Man at the Inipi*

After "The Fire Tender" by Thomas Hubbard

I see you, old man,
standing straight as a ramrod
in respectful pause as you tend
the sacred fire, as you heat
the Grandfather Stones.

I see you, the reverence
you hold for the old ways,
the Tribal ways;
no matter the tribe, they
are your people.

I see you respectfully feed the fire;
smoke curls around you
in a playful embrace. Slowly,
the paunch from too much white
man's beer disappears, the office-
bleached skin reddens, the short
gray hair becomes long and dark.
Loose, it rides free on Grandfather Wind.

I see you, as you reverently slide
the pitchfork under a Grandfather Stone,
carry him to the front of the inipi,
lovingly watch as the woman
brushes away the ash with a
branchlet of holy cedar.

I see you stoop, enter,
place the Grandfather Stone gently
in the holy circle, and with
reverence, back out to
retrieve another.

I see you, and the pain
you accept in order
to pick up the Grandfather Stone,
to carry the Grandfather Stone,
to not drop the Grandfather Stone.

I see you, and your pain fades,
your body becomes young,
healthy, a warrior's body that
once helped paddle a war canoe
across the Salish Sea.

I hear you, as you
offer your voice—young,
strong, clear in an old language
forbidden until mostly lost—
total recovery almost impossible—
to the Great Spirit,
to your inipi brothers and sisters,
and I am blessed

I see you, old man,
standing straight as a ramrod
in respectful pause as you tend
the sacred fire, as you heat
the Grandfather Stones.

* *Inipi ~ Lakota for sweat lodge, means "to live again."*

Of What Does He Dream?

He sleeps but a few minutes
then starts talking in real words
though I can't hear them
well enough to understand.

Sometimes he waits, as if in
conversation before he speaks again.
Other times he speaks
a few words, then quiets.

Is he dreaming? Of what?
Doesn't seem to be nightmares.
He doesn't fidget or
toss about or call out.

He wakes with a smile.

His Bench: An Ekphrastic Poem
Based on a Photograph Not Yet Taken

His bench remains empty
these many days.
The sun shines, the rain drizzles
he is not here to call—
or feed—Henry and Matilda.

I sit on his bench
with a bag of crackers
and homemade cookies.
I rattle the bag, call their names,
still, no crows.

The view is different
from his bench, more expansive.
I feel his presence,
especially as I look toward
my bench, which sits empty.

I lean against his tree,
hold two crackers, close my eyes.
A quiet flutter of wings,
a quiet clack of beaks,
the crackers are taken.

Guilt of the Undying

Oh, god, it's 5 a.m.
I know he's awake, but he's
so still. If I sit, he'll know
I'm awake, then he'll want something.

I'm not awake awake,
If I can get up, go pee, and come
back to bed, without having to do,
to talk, I can go back to sleep

for a bit more shut-eye.
I'm so guilty.
He's dying, I can sleep after he dies.

Every night he wants his desk
set up, so he can work in the morning
without waking me. Every night
I set it up, every night, he says

*no, not this time. I can't get my hand
up to the keyboard, and if I turn
onto my side, I'll knock my computer
to the floor.* Every. Damn. Night!

I'd give everything I own, I am,
if he could turn over
onto his side. Either side.
If he could move,

if he could wrap his arms
around me in a hug,
if he could be without pain.
I don't want him to die.

But part of me wishes he would—
I tell myself it's to end
his pain, but how much is simply
I'm exhausted, need sleep?

I can go ten more days without sleep.
I can wait until he drinks his EOL cocktail.
If the Little Engine could do it, I can do it.
G'morning, Thomas, how went your night?

13

My Fear Is not My Death

A persona poem

The television plays a comedy,
the gals laugh,
I try to follow the show,
but I'm not feeling funny.

I'm gonna die in a couple of days,
I'm scared, but I have to be brave,
can't tell the ladies I'm scared.
It's not death that frightens me,

I don't believe in heaven or hell,
I'll drink the cocktail, fall into
a deep sleep, then a coma, then
I'll die. My fear is I *won't* die;

I'll wake here. No one has ever
come back from death with proof
of what waits for us. I have no memories
before I was born, and I think

when I die, it all just goes black,
blank, nothing. Deep space nothing.
She thinks I'll go to the Ancestors,
I humor her, but I don't think so.

She says she's not afraid of dying,
then admits she's not facing it.
She says she's more curious
than fearful. But admits she doesn't know.

The dialog snuck some lines in.
I'm laughing, feel better.

#

Today's the day! She woke me early
to enjoy my last cup of coffee.
I'm calm. Friends brought my favorite
Rye, and when I took the pre-meds—

anti-nausea and tranquilizer—we all
had a toast to my coming adventure.
And now, the volunteer is here—
she brings the Final Cocktail,

explains once I drink it,
there is no turning back.
Asks if I still want to drink it
"That's why we're all here, ennit?"

Chuckles from all in the room as I down
it in two gulps. Worst. Taste. Ever!
Thumbs up all around, popsicle on a stick,
eyes clo…

The Ringmaster Orchestrates the Acts
A persona poem

Not even five yet.
I'm the only one awake.

The birds are up. But they're no help.
If I had my desk, I could work.

Wake her? Let her sleep?
Aw, hell. She's up enough during the day

fetching me water, making me coffee,
wiping my nose, feeding me.

'Sides I still couldn't work—can't lift my hand
the inch or two needed to reach the keyboard.

I've had a good life,
ALS gives no one a good death.

She's right, my life's a circus. And
I'm a piss poor Ringmaster,

that's what I am. I lie here in bed,
unable to do anything but call out my wants.

Help me, I wanna sit, no I wanna lie back, I gotta
have help to pee, to poop, can't even wipe my ass.

I'm an 85-year-old baby. And nowhere near
as cute as a newborn. Feed me, bring me coffee

use the right straw so I can drink. I control
my life—as long as my voice holds out—

and they do what I ask. My book's
nearly done. Me, too.

When the sun shines, and the pain goes down
I want to live, play in a club again

hold my sax, finger the keys, breathe, watch
the audience enjoy the music, their drinks,

the couple who just discovered each other.
When the sun shines, and the pain goes down,

I know I can get up outta this cursed
prison bed and walk, even dance with a loving

woman in my arms, sing a song
in her ear no one else will hear,

slow dance her to my bed, make beautiful love.
Who am I kidding? Not only does this disease

steal nerves and muscle, it hijacks desire, too. At least
I've got memories. Damn! I don't wanna die.

But I can't go on like this. This ain't living.
It's not even existing. It's *Hell*.

The exit meds are right there, atop
that cabinet. Only three steps, but too far for me.

As if I could stand. As if I could walk.
Arms are too weak to use a walker.

In ten days, they'll be much closer.
In ten days, I'll drink that final cocktail.

In ten days, I, the Ringmaster, will fall into
a deep sleep, then a coma, then when the Ancestors

call me, I will raise my arms and sing and dance
to their embrace. I. Shall. Be. Free.

A'ho!

*A'ho! ~ means thank you. It can also mean amen. It may be used as a greeting or
an ending. It is from many different Native American tribes.*

Lamentations for the Ringmaster

Part 1, May 6

The Ringmaster bounds
into the center ring
doffs his hat with a theatrical flourish
bows to the four directions

Ladies and gentlemen
girls and boys
the Big Top will end
in seventeen nights and a wakeup.

Counting down the days
of the Ringmaster's short-
timer's calendar, do I count
the day of the final exit?

He says seventeen nights and a wake-up.
He chose June 1
but may slide it
in either direction

for he is the Ringmaster
of this circus.
He cannot imagine his non-
existence, can you imagine yours?

The lions and tigers
the bears and elephants
the high-wire acts
the clowns   are all silent

contemplating the end
of life as they know it.
When the Ringmaster leaves,
all will be gone.

A wise teacher told his students,
In death is freedom, for when you
die, you will give away all
of your possessions—

fears, hopes,
shoulds, wants,
pains, loves—
all your belongings.

Part 2, May 16

I watch him die
in increments
and wonder if I
would have such bearing?

I watch
and learn
so, when my time comes,
I will do him proud.

Part 3, May 17

The Ringmaster calls forth
the circus carnivores
to feed them his diet of pain-filled days.

Insulted, they refuse to partake
of his feast, remind him
We only eat pain that we cause.

He must choose his day—
his time—to face
his mortality.
Alone.

The date changes several times
in 24 hours. Again, he looks
at the 30th of this month.

A select few will accompany him
at the start, he must finish
his walk on that path by himself.

The carnivores are happier.
The circus once again
has clowns, high-wire acts

—his pain continues
unwanted, unabated—
and the date is still subject

to change again and possibly
again, and yet again, until the
Eater of Time comes to feast.

Part 4, May 19

Four days since his momentous
and, he says, final decision.

The date has changed
several times, but always

comes back to the 30th. He tells
everyone it will be the 30th,

then changes, in pain,
in agony

with no wait, then remembers
his date affects people

he cares for and about
and many have rescheduled

their lives to accommodate him.
The circus cats smile,

lick their chops in anticipation.
I wonder what I'd do

in the same situation.
It's so easy to be brave

when not required.

Part 5, May 21

The Ringmaster mounts a racing steed,
rides around the ring faster, faster.
No matter the swiftness of his passage,
he cannot speed the departure of time.

He dismounts, and once again directs the acts
as they advance into the tent. The Hospice volunteers
enter as bears wearing frilly collars,
sequined tutus. They hold a glass, a straw

for the Final Exit Cocktail. They dance,
twirl for the audience, the Ringmaster,
call forth the laughter of children, of adults
all for the Ringmaster as his stance wavers.

The high-wire acts watch all below,
the beloved Ringmaster completes his tasks,
smiles for his friends, his family who comprise
the spectators. The bears cease their dance,

run around the ring, wave to the audience,
slow by the Ringmaster, hug him, kiss him,
promise to return on his set date. All is well
in his world, as he remounts the racing horse.

Slowly, the crowd empties the tent, sending hugs
and kisses flying to the Ringmaster. They wait
until they are far from the tent to begin singing
their dirge, begin crying their pain, begin the long moan

of loss. Alone, they vent their grief; in front of him
they remain strong and brave, for their love
of him is unconditional. If he is brave, and can laugh,
then they can too. At least for that short time, he can bless them.

Part 6, May 22

The friends—readers, writers, musicians
gather often in the ring to read,
to sing, to regale the Ringmaster
with words, affection, music.
He sees them as acrobats
swinging from trapeze to trapeze,
flipping at the plot twists,
soaring on the steady bar of the stanza
until they throw themselves off
the platform at the top of the tent
and to the oohs and aaahs
of the spectators, the Ringmaster,
as they realize they hold not the trapeze
but wear wings of bright, shimmery silk
as they soar, birds of beauty, around the tent
to again land on the platform,
again, grab the bar of steel-strong words.
Using their brightly colored wings
now morphed into long scarves,
they weave a shimmery rope as they fall with grace,
land at the Ringmaster's feet.

The audience cheers, stomps,
the risers become a huge drum of joy.
The Ringmaster bows in supplication
to the zeal, the stories, the music in his ears.
He stands, spreads his arms. Tells all he loves us.
And the circus will come no more.
He admonishes all to hold its memory close.
Our sorrows, heavier than the grey circus pachyderms,
lighten because of his compassion,
we are welcomed to float through the heavens in joy,
filled with sunshine, sharing our devotion, our gratitude
with the Ancestors. We know our pain, our loss,
affirmation we live in the lightness of being.
We know healing and ever more love.

Mitakuye Oyasin!

Mitakuye Oyasin! ~ is Lakota and means all are related, all my relations. We are related to each other, to the earth, and all who live upon her or in her waters.

Part 7, May 25

He walks to the center ring,
his stride strong and sure.
With a sweeping bow,
thanks all his friends,
his family new and old
for coming, for partaking in his circus
of poetry, of glass making,
of jamming with fellow musicians,
teaching our beloved youth.

The crowd roars, cheers,
whistles, stomps their allegiance and enthusiasm,
fills his ears,
his heart with love
even as they melt
from his eyes, his ears
into nothingness.
He smiles, at last able to raise
his arms to his Ancestors
as a swirling pillar of white
light envelops him and he dissolves,
leaving only the
barely heard beat of drums,
of horses galloping, chanting
and singing of his tribal people—
in the now empty tent
and his song of happiness—
         All My Relations

Part 8, May 28

The circus is closed.
The Ringmaster asks us,
his caregivers, to allow visitors
by appointment for no more
than 20 minutes, he wishes to sleep.

Tired, bone deep, tuckered out,
he calls his family, tells them goodbye,
tells them he is two days away
from his final exit. Their tears of affection
and loss mingle through the phones.

Visitors understand
it takes strength to die.
Though he never again will attend the circus,
he smiles at the memories.

His sleep fills with dreams,
he speaks them aloud.
His eyes open, he tracks the people
conversing with him.

Once he replied aloud in German.
I looked it up, he spoke it correctly.
When asked, he was shocked.
German, a language he doesn't remember
ever hearing or learning.

He tells me of his dreams,
the ones he remembers, the one
of the many clowns exiting the tiny car.
A sardonic smile upon his face, he asks
Is this all there is?

In my sleep,
I hold him in my arms,
I cry without shame or restraint,
my pillow, salt-rimmed,
I remind him nightly,
we are related,
we are all related.

Part 9, May 30

The Eater of Time
wears his cloak of smoke,
enters the tent,

the tent where the three rings wait,
the carnival animals wait
the audience waits
when brilliant white light tunnels
down, encircles the Ringmaster,
also known as Walks Easy. Smiles.

The Eater of Time,
holds his hand, flat, and blows upon the audience—
in less than a heartbeat,
they are home, at work,
wherever they normally abide,
the Gourmand grins at the animals—
prey and predator alike—
they find themselves in their native habitat;
he throws back his head and whispers a command
only the performers hear,
they, too, are gone to somewhen else.

The ground now naked
of all vestiges of circus,
the Eater, the Gourmand of Time,
embraces the Ringmaster lightly,
whispers in his ear.
The Ringmaster
slides into his final sleep.

A'ho!

Saying Goodbye to Thomas

I.
I want to throw
myself across your bed, across you
to beg, plead
Don't. Please, don't!
We both know you will
why make it harder with my drama?

II.
We share a toast with your favorite Rye
to your new adventure!

III.
We joke and laugh.
When you tell us your fear
waking here
not dying
your bonus sons promise
you will not wake
this side of the veil.
You relax   laughter
again fills the room.

IV.
The time arrives—
in turn, we each hold
your hand, kiss
your face, wish
you safe journey
all while
smiling
holding back our tears.

V.
Your doula, your angel, enters,
carries your final cocktail.

VI.
We all stop breathing.
She gives you the legalities—
There is no antidote.

Drink this and you will die.
Do you wish to change your mind?

VII.
Your answer loud and strong
That's why we're all here, ennit?

VIII.
Two gulps through a large straw.
Worst. Taste. EVER!

IX.
You eat of a popsicle
to kill the taste
to numb your mouth.
At 4 minutes 30 seconds
your eyes roll
to the back of your skull
you finally look toward your new adventure.

X.
I sit next to you, hold your hand
stroke your arm
hope I give you comfort
until your gentle breathing stops
at 2 hours 55 minutes.

XI.
I cannot
release
the
primal
scream
stuck
in my tear-constricted throat.

XII.
My heart shatters
pulses through my body—
a thousand shards
of brittle pain.

XIII.
Who gave you
permission to die?
        I did.

(Bonus sons were his stepsons.)

Your Death, Rehearsed

I rehearsed your death—
           did you know?

First, it was now and
           then, slowly became

weekly and then
           nightly.

Not that I wanted
           you to die—

We both knew
           you would.

No, I rehearsed
           your death

so I wouldn't come
           apart at the seams,

so I wouldn't
           bring shame to you,

to me. It helped,
           I think.

Oh, I still hurt,
           I still cry

but softly. And when
           you breathed your last

as I held your hand,
           softly stroked your arm,

I could barely form
           the words, let alone

force sound out of my tear-
           constricted throat

It's over. And then
    we all cried, held each other.

None of us could find,
    or define, the hole

that suddenly engulfed
    us, the hole

that gave dimension
    to our loss

the hole
    drilled through our hearts.

The Quilt in Back of the Hearse

The last time I saw you
you weren't there. Your body
covered by a blue and white quilt
in the back of the hearse
was empty of you.
It was the last time
I could touch you—
but you weren't there

and I didn't reach out
I didn't kiss you farewell
for the primal scream
was too close to my surface.

I held your hand
for three hours. I softly
stroked your arm for three hours
while you gathered yourself
and quietly made your exit,
leaving all of us who love
you, to learn to live
with the new hole in our hearts
too ragged yet to heal. But!

we have memories
of your love, good times,
touch, of laughter that comes
through our pain
in delightful randomness
to bring us smiles
and chuckles.

I Dreamed Him Alive

Early morning,
before the claxon
of my alarm
I stood in a desert suk
admiring the perfumes
of cinnamon, peppers,
many other spices melded
into that heady bouquet.

A man dressed in white linen slacks,
a white linen shirt, Mexican huaraches,
stood with his back to me.
It was him! My heart skipped,
my breath rushed out of me, my whisper
coarse, barely audible, I spoke his name.

He heard, turned, faced me. A smile
wide and welcoming, lit his face,
his arms spread wide,
I stepped into his embrace.

I don't remember
words spoken, but love
filled our entwinement.
Then he faded,
like smoke from a dry-wood fire.

The feeling in a room

by Thomas Hubbard, the morning after his sister, Sally (Sarah Clark), died.

It's not the walls
defining a room…
they don't change
when one moment
a person is there, and
the next moment is gone
without a door opening
without a window raised.

The same walls remain,
mute, no comment, but
the space… the space
inside the room changes
although words don't come
to explain the difference,
but if we are close
to the person who is gone, or
if we are particularly sensitive
to such things, we sense
a difference.

We can't see the space,
only the things inside, and
like the unchanging walls
the things don't change,
but the space we can't see,
we can feel… and it changes
in that moment, or instant
when a person was there and
the next instant, is gone,
without a door opening
without a window raised.

The space, the invisible space
we can't see, feels different, and
words don't come to explain how
nor is it given us to understand
just how the space changes
inside the walls defining a room

where life escaped, but we who
loved the life that escaped...
we surely... surely feel the change.

We feel it, even from far away, and
we eventually turn and leave, and
we reach out to one another and finally
we close the broken circle, but
we never forget.

Lenora Rain-Lee Good lives eight feet or so from a manmade lake in Kennewick WA. She is the author of four and a third published books of poetry—*Confessions of a Peace Monger* (out of print), *Blood on the Ground* (Redbat Books, 2016), *Marking the Hours* (Cyberwit. net 2020), and *The Bride's Gate and Other Assorted Writings* (Cyberwit.net, 2021). She co-authored *Reflections: Life, the River, and Beyon*d (KDP 2020), with Jim Bumgarner and Jim Thielman, hence "the third." Her poetry has most recently appeared in *Cirque Literary Journal, The Shrub-Steppe Poetry Journal 2024, and Quill and Parchment*, an online Literary Magazine. She is a Pushcart Prize nominee for both poetry and fiction. She writes, quilts, collects & tells terrible shaggy dog stories. Reach her via the Contact form on her website: *https://CoffeeBreakEscapes.com*